From: Lisa

Love '93

Celebrating
Grandmother

Heartland Samplers, Inc.
Edina, Minnesota
Printed in Hong Kong

Celebrating

Grandmother

*The Eskimo has
fifty-two names
for snow because
it is important to
him; there ought to
be as many for love.*

Atwood

*Age does not protect you from love.
But love, to some extent, protects you from age.*

Moreau

The best and most
beautiful things in
the world cannot be
seen or even touched.
They must be felt
with the heart.

Helen Keller

I looked on child rearing not only as a work of love and duty but as a profession that was fully as interesting and challenging as any honorable profession in the world, and one that demanded the best that I could bring to it.

Rose Kennedy

What feeling is so nice as a child's hand in yours? So small, so soft and warm, like a kitten huddling in the shelter of your clasp.

Marjorie

*Love is like a violin.
The music may stop
now and then, but the
strings remain forever.*

Bacher

*A*n archaeologist is
the best husband any
woman can have; the
older she gets, the
more interested he is
in her.

Agatha Christie

Courage looks you
straight in the eye.
The people who told me
it was stern were not
lying; they just forgot
to mention it was kind.

J. Gendler

True strength
is very delicate.

Nevelson

We need time to dream, time to remember, and time to reach the infinite. Time to be.

Gladys Taber

*S*he openeth her
mouth with wisdom;
and in her tongue is
the law of kindness.

Proverbs 31:26

*Grow old along
with me!
The best is yet to be,
The last of life,
for which the first
was made. Our times
are in His hand.*

Robert Browning

It is sad to grow old
but nice to ripen.

Brigitte Bardot

We are always
the same age inside.

Stein

Age is something that
doesn't matter, unless
you are a cheese.

Billie Burke

But to look back
all the time is
boring. Excitement
lies in tomorrow.

Makarova

We never know the
love of the parent
until we become
parents ourselves.

Henry Ward Beecher

*T*reasure each other
in the recognition
that we do not know
how long we shall
have each other.

Joshua Loth Liebman

The head learns new things, but the heart forevermore practices old experiences.

Henry Ward Beecher

*Kindness is a
language the deaf
can hear and the
dumb can understand.*

Seneca

God cannot give us happiness and peace apart from Himself, because it is not there. There is no such thing.

C.S. Lewis

Cheerfulness and contentment are great beautifiers, and are famous preservers of good looks.

Charles Dickens

*T*hose who love
deeply never grow
old; they may die
of old age, but they
die young.

Sir Arthur Wing
Pinero

*R*ose-colored glasses
are never made in
bifocals. Nobody wants
to read the small print
in dreams.

Ann Landers

We often take
for granted the very
things that most
deserve our gratitude.

Ozick

*Nature gives you
the face you have at
twenty; it is up to you
to merit the face you
have at fifty.*

Coco Chanel

*Fortunately for
children, the
uncertainties of
the present always
give way to the
enchanted possibilities
of the future.*

Kirkland

*E*verything else
you grow out of,
but you never recover
from childhood.

        Bainbridge

*E*very morning lean
thine arms awhile
upon the windowsill
of Heaven and gaze
upon the Lord. Then,
with that vision in thy
heart turn strong to
meet the day.

...I have created you and cared for you since you were born. I will be your God through all your lifetime, yes, even when your hair is white with age. I made you and I will care for you. I will carry you along and be your Savior.

Isaiah 4-6:3-4

*E*ven in old age
they will still produce
fruit and be vital.

Psalm 92:14

It's the little things
we do and say
That mean so much
as we go our way.
A kindly deed can
lift a load
From weary shoulders
on the road.

Willa Hoey

The human heart,
at whatever age,
opens to the heart
that opens in return.

Maria Edgeworth

A look of love will, at times, have a better effect than all the prescriptions of a physician on one that ails.

Where there is
room in the heart
there is always room
in the house.

Moore

A child is the
root of the heart.

*Carolina Maria
de Jesus*

A happy family is but an earlier heaven.

Sir John Browning

*There never was
any heart truly great
and generous that was
not also tender and
compassionate.*

South

*One must never
be in haste to end a
day; there are too few
of them in a lifetime.*

Dale Coman

I find life an
exciting business,
and most exciting when
it is lived for others.

Helen Keller

A gentle word,
like summer rain,
May soothe some
heart and banish pain.
What joy or sadness
often springs
From just the
simple little things!

Willa Hoey

*T*o stay young in spirit, keep taking on new thoughts and throwing off old habits.

*Salute the day
with peaceful thoughts,
And peace will fill
your heart;
Begin the day
with joyful soul,
And joy will be
your part.*

Frank B. Whitney

*D*on't regret growing older. It is a privilege denied to many.

*Over the river and
through the wood —
Now grandmother's
cap I spy!
Hurrah for the fun!
Is the pudding done?
Hurrah for the pump-
kin-pie!*

Lydia Maria Child

*The butterfly counts
not months, but
moments, and yet has
time enough.*

*When God measures
a person He puts the
tape around the heart
and not the head.
There is no better
exercise for strength-
ening the heart than
reaching down and
lifting up another.*

I remember,
I remember
How my childhood
fleeted by,
The mirth of its
December,
And the warmth
of its July.

Winthrop Mackworth
Praed

*W*hat do we live for,
if not to make the
world less difficult
for each other?

George Eliot

*Happiness held
is the seed;
happiness shared
is the flower.*

*Some people make
the world more special
just by being in it.*

*W*hen God allows a burden to be put upon you, He will put His arms underneath you to help you carry it.

Ah, the insight of hindsight!

Thurston N. Davis

*L*ove looks not
with the eyes
but with the heart.

If we learn how to give of ourselves, to forgive others, and to live with thanksgiving, we need not seek happiness.
It will seek us.

*Love at first sight
is easy to understand.
It's when two people
have been looking
at each other for
years that it
becomes a miracle.*

This learned I from
the shadow of a tree,
That to and fro did
sway against a wall;
Our shadow selves,
our influence,
may fall
Where we ourselves
can never be.

Anna Hamilton

*O*ver the river and
through the wood,
To grandfather's
house we go;
The horse knows the
way To carry the
sleigh
Through the white
and drifted snow.

Lydia Maria Child

Let the words I speak today be soft and tender for tommorrow I may have to eat them!

...Grandmother's garden was...a productive flower garden...it was a real storehouse of color and odor, out of which one could, day after day, gather rich treasures, and yet leave its beauty apparently undimmed.

Samuel Parsons

*Count your age
by friends — not years.
Count your life by
smiles — not tears.*

*O*ne generation
plants the trees, the
next sits in the shade.

Great occasions for serving God come seldom, but little ones surround us daily. Nothing is so strong as gentleness, nothing so gentle as real strength.

St. Francis de Sales

*What shall I wish
you, dear, today?
That your heart be
happy, bright and gay,
Surrounded by all you
love the best,
And God your pathway
guide and bless?*

Long years you've
kept the door ajar
To greet me, coming
from afar;
Long years in my
accustomed place
I've read my welcome
in your face...

Robert Bridges

Becoming a grandparent is a second chance. For you have a chance to put to use all the things you learned the first time around and may have made a mistake on. It's all love and no discipline.

Dr. Joyce Brothers

*C*hildren have more
need of models than
of critics.

Joseph Joubert

I look into my inmost mind and here her inspiration I find.

Josephine Rice Creelman

*Her heart is
like her garden,
Old-fashioned,
quaint and sweet
With here a wealth
of blossoms,
And there a still retreat.*

Alice E. Allen

Beginning with the highest, the ointment drops even upon those who are unconscious or careless of it, and the whole house is presently filled with its fragrance.

Henry Van Dyke

I'm not a picture-toting grandma — but my grandsons, Tyler J. Phillips and Dean Phillips, just happen to be the best-looking, smartest, best-mannered grandchildren in the continental United States and you can throw in Canada and the Virgin Islands.

Abigail Van Buren

In the man whose childhood has known caresses, there is always a fibre of memory that can be touched to gentle issues.

George Eliot

*T*hose who bring
sunshine to the
lives of others
cannot keep it
from themselves.

James Barrie

*Courtesies of a small
and trivial character
are the ones which
strike deepest in
the grateful and
appreciating heart.*

Henry Clay

You can't light a candle
to show others the way,
Without feeling the
warmth of that bright
little ray;
And you can't give a rose
all fragrant with dew,
Without some of its
sweetness remaining
with you.

*T*o love and be loved
is to feel the sun from
both sides.

David Viscott

We need to learn to
be still in the midst
of activity and to
be vibrantly alive
in repose.

Gandhi

We are never too old to make noo frien's. Frien'ship don't depend on age, but on the kind of a feller you are. A man should keep a boy's heart, an' he'll make frien's like a boy, I don't care ho long his whiskers aer, ner how gray.

Kempton

Youth is not a time of life — it is a state of mind. Nobody grows old by merely living a number of years; people grow old only by deserting their ideals. Years wrinkle the skin, but to give up enthusiasm wrinkles the soul.

The best thing for gray hair is a sensible head.

*T*here is a fountain
of youth: it is your
mind, your talents,
the creativity you
bring to your life.

Sophia Loren

*Granny was so
important to my life,
but for most children
she isn't even around.
That's a loss... I know
my own grandchildren
tell me things they could
not tell their parents.*

*Chase Going
Woodhouse*

*W*ith ten children, I have become a professional worrier, a fact which panics my husband since he read someplace that "worriers tend to die younger than nonworriers." This, of course, is nonsense. If that were true, there wouldn't be any living grandmothers.

Theresa Bloomingdale

A cheerful look brings joy to the heart and good news gives health to the bones.

Solomon

So teach us to number our days, that we may apply our hearts unto wisdom.

Psalm 90:12

*Laughter is a
tranquilizer with
no side effects.*

Were there no God,
we would be in this
glorious world with
grateful hearts and
no one to thank.

Christina Rossetti

*T*rust in the Lord with all your heart and lean not on your own understanding; in all your ways acknowledge him, and he will make your paths straight.

Proverbs 3:5-6

*E*ven to your old age
and gray hairs...
I am he who will
sustain you. I have
made you and I will
carry you; I will
sustain you and I
will rescue you.

Isaiah 46:4

We live in the present,
we dream of the future,
but we learn eternal
truths from the past.
Isn't it splendid to
think of all the things
there are to find out
about? It just makes
me feel glad to be
alive — it's such an
interesting world.

Montgomery

The yesterdays of a
thousand ages have
made us what we are,
and yet it has given
each one the power
to make tomorrow
different from all
of them.

C. M. Stevens

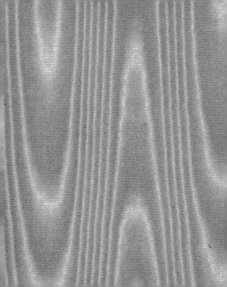